*Dedicated to
the preservation of
our forests...*

THIS BOOK BELONGS TO

© 1989 by Heather Cooper

THE
FOREST
FARMER'S
HANDBOOK

A Guide To
Natural Selection Forest Management

by

Orville Camp

SKY RIVER PRESS
Ashland, Oregon
1984

SKY RIVER PRESS
236 East Main Street
Ashland, Oregon 97520

TABLE OF CONTENTS

PREFACE

I came into forest farming through the back door.

In 1967 I bought 160 acres of logged-over forest land in Selma, Oregon. Everything marketable had been stripped off — it looked like a giant bomb had been dropped on it. All that was left were a few scraggly trees, some stumps and brush, and skid roads running up and down the hills. As a forest it was a disaster, but I was looking at it as a subdivision. I figured I could clean it up to subdivide and make a handsome profit.

To make it look a little better I did some thinning and pruning, cleared and burned some brush, and put some new roads in. By 1971 I noticed a remarkable improvement in some of the stands I had thinned. Whereas the trees had previously averaged about 8'' annual vertical growth, they had suddenly jumped to about 24'' vertical growth! I liked the results so I continued the program. I liked it so much I decided not to subdivide.

By 1978 my forest was beginning to look healthy. The sick trees had either died or recovered, and the smaller trees were now of some value. I had completed over 100 acres of precommercial thinning, and had begun to take out some logs using the same kind of program. By the winter of 1982-83, in addition to logs, we took out nearly 500 cords of firewood — and the health of the forest was steadily improving!

I received a lot of encouragement from local private non-industrial forest owners looking to try something other than monocultural tree farming on their land. Private non-industrial forest land owners have been searching a long time for a simple, logical, economical and ecological approach to forest management. There are no other books or programs that I know of which speak to both the needs of the forest and the needs of the forest farmer. My program is successful, so it was suggested that I write a book about it so that others could benefit from my knowledge and experience. Many forest farmers in my area are now practicing Natural Selection Forest Management on their own lands.

Although I could have made a lot of money from subdividing my property, what good would the money be if I could not buy back what a forest has to offer? Most dedicated forest farmers I know feel the same way.

I had an opportunity to rape the land, sell out, and leave. I didn't. While such a course by one individual might have seemed insignificant, the cumulative effects of many people pursuing that course would be disastrous. I assumed my responsibility for wise conservation and I call on you reading this book to do the same.

Writing a book, I have discovered, is a monumental effort, and one which I could not have accomplished without the help of many dedicated and talented individuals. My editor, Mark Roseland, is a veritable word wizard — he both transformed my cryptic notes into readable English and also shepherded the entire process from conception to publication. Also invaluable were Dean Givens, who took all the photographs on location at Camp Forest Farm; Steve Bohlert of Sky River Press, who engineered the final production stages; Julie Norman for typing and word processing; and Diana Coogle for technical editing.

For friendly criticism and support I am grateful to the Boards of Directors of both the Jackson/Josephine and Illinois Valley Forest Farm Associations, in particular Bill Collins, Art and Paula Downing, Don Sills, and the late Frank Skandera; to Allan Campbell III, Oregon State University Extension Service; to Christopher Bratt, Joan Peterson, Rose Cretney, Wallace Pollard, Joe Stancar; and to my father, Orville Camp, Sr.

Special thanks are also in order to Art Wilson, Bill MacKenzie, Wes Brown, Gordon Borchgrevink, Bill James, Marty Main, Bobcat, Roger Schuessner, and many others too numerous to mention here.

Last but in no way least I am thankful to those who have had to put up with me at home during this process, my wife Rachel and my children Mark, Corinthia and Cameron. It is with the hope of leaving a better world for them that I wrote these pages.

Orville Camp
March, 1984

INTRODUCTION

Our forests are in trouble. Poor management and conservation practices have the public up in arms. People can *see* that something is wrong. Forests, perhaps our greatest renewable natural resource, have not been renewing. Conservation is supposed to mean the wise use of the earth and its resources. It's high time for us to get wise.

Nearly half of my home state of Oregon, about 30.7 million acres, is covered with forests. Of this, over 75%, or some 24 million acres, are capable of growing commercial timber. (Commercial forest land by state law means conifer or softwood timber forests growing timber such as Douglas fir.)

Oregon's forest products are valued at some $5 billion annually and employ more than 90,000 people; they have furnished the building materials for one out of every six homes built in the U.S.; and they have been far and away the state's most valuable economic asset.

Yet, even though Oregon's forests have one of the highest timber producing potentials per acre on earth, *timber shortages and declines are expected*. Studies of Oregon's future timber supply forecast a decline in harvest volume over the next 30 years. In fact, unless there are changes in current policies and procedures, the harvest level in western Oregon, where most of the timber is located, is expected to decline *up to 22%* by the year 2000.* Similar declines are forecast for other states.

Our leaders, rather than examining *why* this situation exists and what can be done about it, are instead now trying to develop and attract other (mostly "high-technology") industries — which are

---

*From "Timber for Oregon's Tomorrow" , a study prepared for the Oregon State Board of Forestry by the Forest Research Laboratory at Oregon State University under the direction of Dr. John Beuter.

dependent on resources from other places to stay alive. As a state, indeed as a nation, our real wealth depends upon our natural resources, so it is not hard to understand why our quality of life is rapidly deteriorating. These leaders say we must "diversify" our economy to buffer ourselves against the ups and downs of the forest industry. Hogwash! Forests are what we have here! Our forests have more potential diversity than all the other industries under consideration combined! *Let's diversify the forest industry!*

Nearly 61% of Oregon's commercial woodlands are managed for the public by government agencies. Most of the public timberlands are classified as National Forests and are managed by the U. S. Forest Service. A large amount of public land is also managed by the Bureau of Land Management. The state, counties and cities manage smaller percentages. Only 39% of this land belongs to private owners, and of this the majority, or 21%, is owned by the timber products industry, leaving 18% for the private nonindustrial sector spread out among 25,000 landowners.

The timber industry, with its extensive network of laws, taxes, schools, etc., has been somewhat like a big dinosaur. At its present rate of evolution it has been very slow to try new kinds of solutions — even in the face of old kinds of problems. It is the private nonindustrial sector, the forest farmers, you and I, who can demonstrate an alternative, holistic approach to healthy forestry. We can model a different method, and a different spirit, on our forest farms.

We must realize that the forests are not just trees to be managed but rather a complex ecosystem which includes humans. As participants in this ecosystem we are not aware of most relationships within it; many that we are aware of we do not understand and, quite possibly, we never will. Still, the more knowledgeable we become the better our forests can be managed.

When we substantially alter or remove any part of the ecosystem we open the door to a series of troubles. When we try to correct a problem with unnatural methods we open the door to even more problems, which multiply with each unnatural check until everything is quite out of control. Then we lose our forests.

It may take many years for this chain of effects to run its course (trees can take 100 years or longer to completely die) and so we may not see it or recognize it for a while, but it does take place. Today in our forests the unnatural massive use of chemicals and the impacts of poor harvesting techniques allow us to see these effects: deterioration in the quality of our water, loss of wildlife, the increasing spread of unchecked insect and disease problems, destruction of predator habitats, the continuous failure to get forest land back into production...the list runs on and on. And, because the forest environment deteriorates, so does the human environment.

Natural Selection Forest Management, as presented here, is an all-age, all-species management system which could open the door to a much more complete and responsible forest management system by the entire industry. How well the forest ecosystem can be maintained or improved while harvesting and managing is limited only by the knowledge and understanding one has of the forest ecosystem and the ecological succession of the forest. Natural Selection Forest Management should economically maintain or improve the ecosystem and thus increase the sustained yield per acre. This, in turn, would improve both our economy and our environment.

It is important to note that Natural Selection Forest Management is not just a "tree farm" management system; rather, it is a system of "forest farm" management, and there is a world of difference between the two! A tree farm is managed primarily for trees as a specialized crop and the ecosystem is usually addressed only as necessary to support the growing of that specialized crop, just like hay or any other agricultural product. With Natural Selection Forest Management, the health of the total forest ecosystem is addressed as the priority. Emphasis may be placed on certain more valuable products for human use, but the checks and balances of the ecosystem remain the priority.

TREE FARMING   vs.   FOREST FARMING

conventional forest management	Natural Selection Forest Management
trees as cash crop	many income-producing products
agricultural production model	forest ecosystem model
short term	sustainable
man in charge of needs	Nature in charge of needs
burning, chemicals used on vegatation and pests	no burning usually, no massive use of chemicals
clearcuts	selective harvesting

Natural Selection Forest Management uses natural selection methods for harvesting various products. The products we harvest to serve our needs are the ones selected by Nature for removal. This is the only time-tested and proven method of sustainable forestry.

As business people we are of course interested in profit, but we in the Northwest need not be blinded by the timber industry's insistence on conifers as the only profitable product in the forest. A properly tended forest yields many useful products: lumber, firewood, hardwood for furniture, poles, fenceposts, mushrooms, huckleberry brush, etc. It has other uses as well — recreation, education, wildlife habitat, etc. A well-managed forest farm can be profitable to the owner and at the same time provide an environment of great pleasure. It is the hope of this author that you will find this book useful in the sensible and profitable management of your forest and that the forest ecosystem will thrive not only in your forest and in mine but in all the great forests of this country and of the world.

THE FOREST FARMER

Personal Goals:

In developing a forest management plan, the first considerations are your personal goals and desires. The following is a list of key questions that will help you determine your goals and desires, though there may be other questions unique to your situation which you will also want to ask yourself.

Questions to ask yourself

- What do I want from my forest?
- Do I want my forest to be a good financial investment?
- Would I like my forest to be income-producing? If so, would I like to receive that income annually or periodically over time? How much income do I expect?
- Would I like my forest to be a kind of savings account for emergencies?
- Do I want to create a valuable forest estate to serve my family and heirs?
- Do I want my forest to be more attractive?
- Do I want a healthy forest?
- Is my goal to be able to live in a forest-like environment?
- Is my goal to both live and work in the forest?
- Do I want to use my forest for recreational purposes?
- Do I want an abundance of wildlife living in harmony in my forest?
- Do I want Nature's plants and animals to do my forest management? And I do the harvesting to serve my needs?
- Do I want to grow just one particular crop, such as Douglas-fir trees, for example, and eliminate all competition for food and space?
  (If you answer yes to this last question, this book is not written for you — you are interested in tree farming, not forest farming.)

Personal Restrictions

Will I like Forest Farming?

If you don't like being in the woods, think twice about going into forest farming.

You need to ask yourself some hard questions, and answer them honestly — if you don't, the truth will catch up with you later. Are you basically a city dweller? A country hick? A small town type? This is important, because if you are not happy where you live, you will find it difficult to be successful at your work.

You might choose to work out a compromise, at least for a while, between full time forest farming and city dwelling or other kinds of employment and lifestyles. This can also reduce your risks. You can try your hand at forest management while predominantly making your living at some other profession. If that works out, then you may decide to become a full time forest farmer. Forest farming is like any other business. You must have the expertise. You must know how to run a business. And you must know how to sell your products. If you do not know some part of these three requirements, you will need to hire it out.

Will I make a good forest farmer?

Do you have the necessary time, knowledge, expertise, stamina and physical health necessary to accomplish your goals? You may need to make many compromises! If you are limited in any of these ways, you may need to contract part or all of your management tasks to someone else. This may help you, or hinder you, in achieving your goals. If you do elect to contract out part or all of your forest management, make sure that you or the person you hire has a good understanding of *how* the forest works. You cannot manage successfully if you do not understand what you are doing. Like any other business, success demands that you learn about the obstacles you will need to overcome.

Do I have enough money to do what I want to do?

One of the prime considerations in the accomplishment of your goals is the usual one, money. Do you have money enough to purchase the kind of property it will take to fulfill all of your personal goals? After you own the property, do you have the capital that will be necessary to carry out your objectives? This is the point where big compromises are often made.

Is forestry a sound financial investment in my area?

Business and financial institutions must be assured that the forest and the forest farmer are a stable and sound investment. In order for this to occur, the private forest economic base must be large enough to sustain harvesting crews and specialized manufacturing facilities for all those various products, as well as their marketing. The economic base must be large and sound enough for all those businesses in order for them to invest with security in the necessary ingredients such as equipment, time and knowledge. Subsequently, your investment potential will hinge very highly on considerations in conjunction with taxes and land use planning. Check with lending institutions and other investors in your area, Use their experience and expertise. Also check with your local State Extension Forester and/or Service Forester if you have them.

Other Restrictions

What deed restrictions do I have either directly on my land or adjoining my land?

There may be certain legal restrictions on your land or on adjoining land that would hamper some of your management operations. Such restrictions might prohibit the harvesting of timber or the cutting of any of forest products or the building of roads; they might limit the use of roads or prohibit the hauling of forest products over roads. Noise level restrictions often occur when forest land is close to a residential development.

The best access for marketing your forest products is a well-designed and well-constructed system of access roads, provided your forest land restrictions permit it. Some of these restrictions are streams, rock outcroppings, swamps, fragile soils, buildings, fences, slopes, aspect, and impact upon forest wildlife and habitats. These operational restrictions may become very significant in terms of accomplishing your personal goals.

Does Natural Selection Forest Management apply to any size forest?

Yes. Regardless of the size of your forest, Natural Selection Forest Management can still address many of your forest's needs and your personal goals. However, the size of your forest acreage can greatly affect the management restrictions imposed by those necessities, Time and Money.

Your first major compromise may be in the size and quality of forest you can afford to purchase. Beyond a certain point, the smaller the unit, the more difficult it becomes to satisfy the forest's needs and your personal goals. Some common forest management considerations include acreage, stocking, age, yield potential of trees and other plants, adequate habitats for all natural wildlife, recreation potentials, access roads, and so on. You need a parcel of forest land of adequate size to justify the expenditures for equipment or contracting you will make in order to manage and harvest forest products. It is hard to imagine a highly successful operation with less than one full-time (and devoted!) person to manage a forest farm. If your forest land is of adequate size to sustain both you and your forest, you will find you can manage it more economically.

Since Natural Selection Forest Management is an all-species plant and animal forest management system, it follows that the habitats of all species of plants and animals in your forest must be protected and preserved. Habitat size requirements vary with different species, and particularly with their position in the food chain. Secondary consumers, like hawks or mountain lions, which eat other animals, may require up to 100 square miles or more for an adequate habitat. Primary consumers, like deer, which eat green plants, may require less than one square mile because of the greater quantity of food available. When a forest is deteriorating, the first species of wildlife to disappear will usually be the secondary consumers.

Can I manage a small tract profitably?

Parcel size is quite relative to profitability; smaller tracts are sometimes managed to produce more profit per acre, but only up to a point. As size decreases a threshhold is reached where Nature's ability to manage for you is reduced and so your management costs will rise.

The size of a forest farm, in conjunction with the surrounding area, must be large enough to sustain all forms of life within the forest community. If your land is too small for forest farming you will pay a heavy price to sustain it — as is easily observed near urban areas.

A major consideration for the forest landowner is whether you can justify the cost of purchasing necessary management and harvesting equipment. Or if you contract it out, will the return on your forest products offset the costs of moving in equipment?

My own personal experience in southwestern Oregon is that anything less than 160 acres of good forest land becomes increasingly less profitable, and I know of few people with economically successful management on less than 40 acres. The poorer the land, of course, the larger an area you will need for economic viability. However, this is not to say that you should not manage smaller parcels, especially in a forest area, because each part does indeed affect the whole — every step you take to improve the health of your forest improves the health of all adjoining forests, and ultimately improves our health as well.

20

Especially with a small tract, good land use planning practices that protect your forest investment from real estate speculators and subdividers (the short-term profit people) are crucially important. You must know how much protection you have against this. What is the history of land use planning in your area? Forestry is a lifetime investment. If the real estate people are going to put you out of business, I'd say it's a poor investment. You might as well join them and then move out because your forest and your forest profitability will rapidly deteriorate. Your rights to life, liberty, and the pursuit of happiness as a forest farmer will only be a dream.

What are the impacts of other management systems?

Agricultural or monocultural operations, such as tree farming, can be a serious threat to forest farming. Monocultural farming, which means growing one principal crop, usually results in the elimination of most of the natural plants and animals that we encourage in forest farming. If you are bordered by a monocultural farming operation which employs management techniques such as aerial herbicide or pesticide spraying, you will want to think more than twice about the potential threat to your forest farm — and to your family.

Past management and harvesting techniques can have a tremendous impact on the cost of re-establishing a healthy, profitable forest crop. Though forest land is typically rated by soils, specifically to soils as they pertain to conifer tree stocking, this often has little bearing on how productive your forest land will be during your lifetime. If the soils are good, and the previous crop was good, this is not necessarily an indication that the next crop of the same trees will be good, since climate, soil and water determine the kinds of plants that can grow there. You can observe the areas where desirable seedlings and mature trees are growing to determine whether climate, soil and water conditions are favorable. If you live in southern Oregon, for example, and the previous crop was clearcut, the forest climate may have been so drastically altered that the cost of re-establishing the same crop could be prohibitive.

Without adequate stocking, it will be a long time before your forest will yield an abundance of forest products; a newly-planted forest may take 50-100 years or even longer to reach its capacity. You need to know the ages and sizes of the various trees and other marketable plants in order to project your potential yield.

Do I have a market already available for all my forest products or will I have to establish some or all of them?

You will need to know if you can market your forest products, where to market them, and what the costs will be to do so. There usually is a market for various saw logs, but do you have a market for small poles and firewood? Small products such as huckleberries, burls, odd wood shapes, manzanita and other foliage used for floral decorations can also be highly profitable.

The availability of markets also depends on how many others are managing a forest in your area. Processing plants, for example, will not set up production unless there is enough forest potential in your area to support them and enough producers to supply them.

Is my forest land protected by sound land use planning and zoning laws?

Good planning is the process of guiding the development of an area in order to preserve our rights to life, liberty and the pursuit of happiness. Simply increasing the population of an area eats away at these rights so additional rules are necessary in order to protect them. Good planning can beautify and protect our communities and make life more comfortable, enjoyable and profitable by protecting our forest resource lands.

Zoning is the implementation and enforcement of land use planning by law. This is done in Oregon by each city and county, and by the state Land Conservation and Development Commission (LCDC). It may be very difficult for you as a forest farmer to turn your forest farm into residential development, for example, but for the real estate speculator and developers there are usually loopholes. You may not see them, but a good test is when you see development going on in forest resource land in your area, then you know that loophole exists. Throughout our state and nation good forest land is continually being removed and converted to development.

Do your local land use planning and zoning laws protect your forest from conflicting uses on adjoining property? For example, if a neighbor dislikes the noise created on your forest farm, from your management, whose rights prevail — your neighbor's rights to quiet or your rights to be a forest farmer?

How do taxes affect my forest farming?

Many factors determine the actual amount of taxes you have to pay, which of course affects the amount of money you will have for forest management and, therefore, your management effectiveness.

Land use planning and zoning have a tremendous impact on taxation. If your land is to be used for development instead of for forestry it will have a higher short term value and be taxed accordingly. In my area, smaller forest tracts have a much higher tax rate per acre than

A (madrone) hardwood forest community

larger tracts because of the way they are taxed. Forest lands are supposed to be taxed according to their ability to produce forest products. If your land is zoned as agricultural, *all* of it is taxed according to your soil's ability to grow crops. If the same land is zoned forest, however, you will have a parcel of land taken out where your home is and taxed like a city lot — and that's in addition to the rest of the forest land taxation rate.

In Oregon, the classification of your land as "forest" for taxation purposes or for management assistance is determined by the stocking of conifers such as Douglas-fir for timber purposes. You may have the best land in the world for growing hardwood trees — it doesn't count and the law doesn't care. You will not be eigible for forestry taxation benefits unless you have a minimum stocking of timber-producing conifer species.

As an Oregon forest farmer you are subject to something called a severance tax. If you are harvesting agricultural crops such as hay, corn, carrots, fruit, etc., you do not have to pay a tax on them as you sell them. If your crop is considered a forest crop, however, you are liable for a 6 1/2% severance tax whether you make money or lose money when you sell your products. This means that when you are thinning your forest crops, which may be costing you money, and selling some of that thinned material as, say, firewood, you will be penalized at the rate of 6 1/2% of market value for trying to merely recover some of your costs. This is a major factor to think about when considering how to recover your forest management costs.

In my area, a popular program among forest farmers is the thinning and removal of competing vegetation in a pre-commercial timber stand. This may cost in the vicinity of $100 per acre. If you cut this excess growth into firewood and sell it instead of wasting it, your costs are reduced and the thinning program becomes more affordable. But . . . when you sell this firewood you become liable for a 6 1/2% severance tax based upon its market value.

Another kooky tax is fire patrol. In Oregon you pay for this public service in two ways: 1) the local fire department, which covers your house and structures; and 2) the State, which covers your forest land. This situation is peculiar to forestry.

Then there's transportation. As an agricultural farmer you are eligible for farm plates to serve the needs of hauling your products to market. As a forest farmer, however, if you haul your firewood to market in the same manner you may be subject to a much higher licensing fee and be required to purchase special PUC plates *and* be taxed an additional fee based on mileage. This can be very expensive!

All of these taxes I've been talking about apply whether or not you make a profit! If you do happen to make a profit, then you are subject to what everyone else pays, state and federal income taxes.

In summary, our forest taxation laws encourage development for other purposes. In the state of Oregon and elsewhere we are paying a very heavy price for this. We are rapidly losing both the productivity of our forest land and also the forest itself!

What laws affect Forest Farming?

There are forestry laws, and then there are other laws on the forestry laws, and then there are still other laws that affect forestry that are not forestry laws.

Forestry laws are difficult to grasp. First of all, I don't know of a single one that clearly defines a forest in terms of management. Local, state, and national laws all use different definitions and terminology, depending on the concern of that law, for example, land use, taxation, or management.

There are some other laws you need to know about, such as the Oregon Forest Practices Act, which concerns harvesting, road construction or maintenance, soil and erosion control measures, slash disploant, stream protection, waste disposal, yarding and skidding, and notification of equipment operations in the forest. You should be able to obtain the necessary information from your State Department of Forestry. Oregon also has labor laws which require licensing and bonding of contractors or, if you hire someone to work for you, very high insurance or Workmen's Compensation rates.

You need to know about these laws. Some of them can severely handicap your ability to successfully manage a forest farm. Some of the forest land in southwestern Oregon, for example, is simply not suitable for Douglas-fir tree farming. Trying to establish this kind of forest where nature could not is usually prohibitively expensive and ecologically stupid.

Where can I obtain technical assistance for Forest Farming?

I know of no sources of technical assistance for all-age, all-species forest management. You can get *some* help from your State Department of Forestry's Service Forester and your State University Forestry Extension Agents. These people are usually very helpful within their limitations (determined by their superiors), but their orientation is toward conifer tree farming.

It is interesting to note that forestry school graduates often begin their careers as State Service Foresters. In order to advance, however, they must typically move out of this role, and so their experience and expertise are lost to the forest farmer.

The Schools of Forestry throughout the land are really improperly named. They should be called the Schools of Tree Farming, because that is what their students are trained in. Graduates almost always go to work in the *timber* processing industry or else the government in some timber-related capacity. Consequently most of our foresters are not really foresters at all but rather single-age, monocultural tree farm specialists — converting our private, industrial and public forest lands into conifer tree farms.

What educational resources are available to help me learn more about all-age, all-species forest management?

Many progressive foresters have been talking for years about theories of forest management like single-tree selection. More recently some have even begun using terms like ''all-age, all-species'' and ''natural selection'' , but methods for practicing these ideas have not been readily available to the public, and they are assuredly not currently in the vocabulary of most government and industrial foresters. As forest farmers we are trying to bring these methods and ideas into public view. I know of no other written materials on the practice of Natural Selection Forest Management — that's why I wrote this book. A good ''people resource'' , however, is your local Forest Farm (or Small Woodlands) Association. Check with your State Extension Forester and/or Service Forester if you have trouble locating your Forest Farm Association.

THE LIVING FOREST

What is a forest? We normally think of forests as large areas of land covered with trees, but they are more than that. A forest includes many smaller plants such as shrubs, mosses, wildflowers, fungi, and microscopic plants. In addition, many kinds of animals make their home in the forest, including birds, insects, reptiles, and mammals. Millions of life-forms exist in the forest. Most of them cannot survive in an environment other than the forest.

Forest Structure

Every forest has various layers of plants. The five basic ones, from the highest to the lowest, are the canopy, the understory, the shrub layer, the herb layer, and the forest floor.

The tops of the tallest dominant trees in the forest make up the *canopy*. This layer receives full sunlight. As a result, it produces more food than does any other layer. Many birds, animals, fungi and insects live in the canopy, where they take advantage of this food.

Shorter trees that grow beneath the canopy form the *understory*. The understory trees receive less sunlight than do the trees of the canopy, and therefore produce less food. Some trees in the understory may eventually join the canopy layer. Others, such as the yew tree, may require the special climate created as a result of the canopy to grow well. However, the understory provides sufficient food as well as shelter for many kinds of forest wildlife.

The *shrub layer* consists mainly of shrubs — that is, woody plants which, unlike trees, have more than one stem. Shrubs do not grow as tall as trees. Many kinds of birds and insects live in the shrub layer. A forest with an open canopy and understory tends to have a much heavier shrub layer than one with a dense canopy.

Small, soft-stemmed plants, such as ferns, grasses, wildflowers, and tree seedlings make up the *herb layer*. This layer receives limited sunlight, but even in forests with dense layers above, enough sunlight reaches the ground to support some herb growth. The herb layer is the home of forest animals that live on the ground, such as insects, mice, snakes, deer, bears, and coyotes.

The *forest floor* includes the soil, and serves as the dumping area for all of the forest layers above. It is covered with animal droppings, leaves, twigs, and dead plants and animals. The forest floor is home for an incredible number of small living organisms such as earthworms, fungi, insects, bacteria, and other microscopic life. These organisms break down or decompose the waste materials into basic chemical nutrients necessary for new plant growth; they depend upon the upper layers for food and for the moderation of climate necessary to sustain them.

Each layer of the forest structure serves to modify physical influences such as light intensity, light quality, temperature, wind velocity, relative humidity and evaporation rate as they filter down through the forest canopy, the understory, the shrub layer, the herb layer, and finally into the soil on the forest floor. At the top, the forest canopy receives the full force of weather. At the bottom, in the soil, light is absent and the temperature and moisture are relatively stable in contrast to higher forest layers.

Each forest layer creates its own climate which determines the kinds of green plants that can live there. The food, shelter, and habitat provided by those green plants will in turn determine the number and kinds of other species that can live there. The climate, therefore, within each forest layer and throughout all the layers is the major controlling factor in determining the species representation and population of all plants and animals.

A *population* is a group of individuals of the same species that live within a given location. Individuals of more than one species interacting in a unique way in a given location constitute a *community*. Communities may form within each layer of the forest structure; for example, the herb community is made up of mammals, tree seedlings, reptiles, insects, etc., and the forest floor community is comprised of earthworms, fungi, bacteria, etc.

We can think of a population as, say, all the people living in a neighborhood; whereas a community would include not only all the people but also their houses, food sources, pets, plants, etc. in that neighborhood. Both the human and the forest communities are constantly changing in appearance (think of the forest in autumn or in spring), but both have structures and functions which can be studied and described, and which are unique attributes of the group. Each also has a unique (ecologists call it "peculiar") organization of plant and animal life which, while distinct, is also dependent on adjoining communities and the major community, just like neighborhoods in a city.

When a forest community is relatively self-sustaining and self-regulating, it is called a *major community*. Within a major forest community are innumerable smaller communities which, while not themselves self-sustaining, combine to make up a major community. For example, a hole in a decaying log may represent a community, which is also part of a larger forest layer community (the herb layer community), which is also part of the five layers of the forest community which together make up a still larger community on an acre of ground with unique climate, soil, and water conditions. Now consider that it may take thousands or even millions of acres of forest to become a major community!

Combine all these communities within all the living and nonliving things in a given place and you can see we have one of the most complex levels of organization in nature, a *forest ecosystem*.

A forest ecosystem can be divided into six main parts, based on the relationship of energy and food in the system. (1) The *sun* supplies the energy necessary to sustain all forms of life on earth. (2) *Abiotic substances*, or nonliving factors such as sunlight, climate, soil, and water are needed to support (3) *primary producers*, or green plants, which change the light energy of the sun into chemical energy in plant protoplasm (cell material). This energy is transferred in the form of food. Then, (4) *primary consumers*, (animals, for example) eat the plant and change the chemical energy again into animal protoplasm. It changes again if the animal dies and its body rots, and bacteria and other small organisms in the soil break down the compounds into simple nutrients. These go back into the soil, and growing plants take them in through their roots as food. Or, a primary consumer, such as a mouse, may be eaten by a (5) *secondary consumer*, such as a hawk. When a forest's condition is deteriorating, secondary consumers are usually the first to go. When the last animal in the food chain dies, (6) *decomposers*, such as bacteria and fungi, break down its body into simple nutrients. Decomposers also break down dead plants. The nutrients from the decomposing bodies and plants then go back into the soil and are used again by plants.

One of the most important laws of Nature is that energy can neither be created nor destroyed. In other words, you can't get something out of nothing — nor can you get nothing out of something! When a gopher eats a garden plant, the plant vanishes from sight, but the energy that was the plant does not vanish from the earth. When the gopher, in turn, is eaten by a hawk, the gopher is gone, but the energy that was the gopher does not disappear. The life energy that the gopher embodied continues in a new form, in this case the form of the hawk. This series of stages that energy goes through in the form of food is called a *food chain*. Some energy is "lost" in the form of heat, as it passes down the chain. Therefore the volume of primary consumers, for example, is much less than the volume of plants needed to support them.

A food chain may follow many different pathways. Few ecosystems have a simple, linear food chain. Forest ecosystems are made up of many different producers, consumers, and decomposers. Energy passes from one to another in many different food chains. This network of food chains is called a *food web*. The more diverse and complex the food web, the more stable (unchanging) the ecosystem. This is why a forest community consisting of a wide variety of plants and animals will remain more consistent in its structure than one in which a harvesting program has removed much of this variety.

The Three Essentials: Climate, Soil & Water

As a forest develops, it continuously changes the climate, soil and water available and therefore the kinds of plants and animals that can live there. This series of changes is known as "ecological forest succession" . It may take millions of years for a forest to evolve into the forms we find in our forests today.

In the forest, all plants and animals are interdependent to various degrees. We too, are dependent on the forests, not only for our economy, but for our environment and our enjoyment as well.

Forest climate is the key to forest health. As described earlier, forest climate (which includes light intensity, light quality, temperature, wind velocity, relative humidity and evaporation rate) is affected by many factors. The forest farmer doesn't have much influence on the climate above the forest canopy, but below the canopy various forest practices can make a difference. Poor harvesting methods, for example, can severely alter the forest climate, wreaking a devastating impact on both the balance of nature and on the ability of the forest community to sustain many different forms of life. Removal of even a single tree can have a significant impact on forest climate, depending on its position in the forest structure. When a plant is selected for harvesting, or when a large number of plants are harvested, the forest farmer must be careful not to change the forest climate to such an extent that it upsets the checks and balances of Nature.

The forest climate also affects the soil and its ability to support the various plants and animals of the forest community. Decomposers are the plants and animals, chiefly fungi and bacteria, that live by extracting energy from the decaying tissues of dead plants and animals. In the process they release simple chemical compounds, making them available to plants. These nutrients are essential for green plants. The ability of the soil to sustain green plants and animals depends upon the ability of these decomposers to continue supplying the needed nutrients. These decomposers, in turn, are dependent on the forest climate for their survival.

Water, so essential for every living thing, is stored in the soil, in the air, in plants and in animals. The forest climate affects each individual's ability to store moisture and so in turn affects the ability of forest plants and animals to survive drought. The forest farmer's harvesting process must leave the forest climate in a condition which enables the forest ecosystem to store sufficient moisture to sustain itself.

All of the living and non-living things in the forest have some kind of water storage ability. Together they store tremendous amounts of water for long periods of time. This serves to sustain the forest through periods of drought. There are many ways that plants and animals can store water. Plants, for example, store it in their stems and leaves, in the soil with their roots, on the forest floor in dead wood, and in addition they help keep it from evaporating by substantially cooling the area below the canopy on hot summer days.

The Four Basic Needs of Forest Plants and Animals

All living organisms in the forest have certain basic needs which must be met to ensure their survival as individuals and as species. These needs apply equally to forest plants (trees, shrubs, flowers, etc.) and to forest animals. The four basic needs are food, habitat, shelter, and reproduction.

Food

All forest plants and animals must have food for nourishment, yet only green plants can make their own food. They capture sunlight with chlorophyll, which enables carbon dioxide from the air to unite with water and minerals from the soil to create food. The oxygen they give off is the source of the atmospheric oxygen we breathe. Therefore, all other plants (like mushrooms, for example) and animals ultimately depend upon green plants for their food.

Habitat

The habitat of an organism is the place where it lives, or where you would go to look for it. It is its address. Habitat can also refer to the place occupied by an entire community. Every habitat limits both

31

the kinds and the number of things that live there, but a natural habitat may satisfy the needs of many kinds of plants and animals.

Shelter

Animals must have a place for rest and recuperation, a place that is protected or sheltered from their enemies or from a harsh environment. Most forest plants also need protection or shelter during part or all of their lives.

Reproduction

Reproduction is the process by which we create more of our own kind. The survival of all species of life forms depends on reproduction.

Climate and weather have both long- and short-term effects on such things as courtship behavior, mating time, egg-laying, and development in the immature stages of life. Most higher forms of plant life are pollinated by environmental agents, such as wind or insects.

These four basic needs make a great argument for preserving snags. Snags are used for protection from weather, communications (singing, drumming, calling), resting, roosting, food storage, exterior nesting, cavity nesting, and hunting perches. In Oregon and Washington at least 74 species use snags for reproduction, at least 44 species use snags for feeding, and at least 187 species (of birds, mammals, amphibians and reptiles) use dead and down logs for cover, feeding, reproduction or other survival needs.

The Balance of Nature — Checks and Balances

In any given area of the forest you will find many kinds of plants and animals. As discussed earlier, within any one of these areas all the members of one species make up a population. The size of each population stays fairly stable unless some disaster alters conditions in the area. Ecologists refer to this stability of population size as the *balance of nature*.

Any change in one part of a natural community — such as an increase or decrease in the population of a species of plant or animal — causes reactions in other parts of the community. Most of the time, these reactions work to restore the balance.

For instance, the relationship among plants, rabbits, and hawks can be illustrated by looking at an ecosystem that includes these three organisms. A rabbit needs air and water from its physical environment to breathe and drink. It also needs biological features, such as plants, for food and shelter. On one side of the food chain, rabbits are eaten by hawks and other flesh-eating predators. On the other side of

A snag provides food, habitat, shelter and reproduction for many different species of wildlife.

the food chain, certain parasites live in and on the rabbits. Furthermore, each rabbit eats food and uses cover that another rabbit could have eaten and used.

Let us assume that, during a certain year, the temperature and rainfall within this ecosystem are ideal for plant growth. As a result, the rabbits have a more plentiful supply of food than usual. The females are healthy and well-fed, and they have large, healthy litters. The young rabbits have enough food, and nearly all of them survive. The rabbit population grows.

Soon the area becomes overrun with rabbits. They must compete with one another for food and shelter. The losers become weak and unprotected, and may fall victim to disease and parasites. They also become easy targets for hawks, so the rabbit population decreases.

To the hawks, more rabbits means more food. The hawks respond in much the same way as the rabbits to an increased food supply

— their population grows — but as secondary consumers their population growth is not as rapid. Still, more hawks means more rabbits are hunted, and so the number of rabbits continues to shrink. The rabbit population decreases until it once again comes into balance with the community's ability to support it. This illustrates nature's system of *checks and balances*. Here are the other factors involved:

Competition

A community has limited amounts of the food and shelter necessary for any given population. Therefore, individual members of that population must compete for those necessities. Members of different populations with similar food or shelter requirements also must compete, but less intensely than those competing within populations.

Predators

Predators actually help the population of their prey — *if* the two species have lived in the same ecosystem for a long time. Under such conditions the prey species learns to deal with the predator. Therefore, the predator normally kills only the weakest and least desirable members of the prey group. This keeps the prey population in a healthy condition.

Diseases and Parasites

Diseases and parasites can reduce or even wipe out a population. But most diseases and parasites are not like the Hong Kong flu coming in from foreign shores to wipe out unsuspecting organisms. Usually they've been around for most of the life history of the host (infected) species, and the host species — when it's in a healthy condition — has adapted to living with them. Like predators, then, disease and parasites serve as important population controls, primarily in the presence of other factors, such as competition for food or shelter.

Behavior

Among some plant and animal populations, behavior helps govern population size. There are three major behavioral factors which influence a population in this way: (1) territory, (2) dominance, and (3) stress.

Territory is the requirement among certain populations of plants and animals for a minimum amount of space — regardless of the available food or shelter. Among such species, one plant or animal or a group of plants or animals establishes a territory. No other members of the species are allowed in this area, and breeding is usually restricted to those with territories. This behavior ensures that the strongest members of the population — those plants and animals that have territories — will have food and produce offspring.

Dominance occurs among many types of plants and animals. Within such populations, the stronger individuals dominate the weaker ones. These dominants get the best food, shelter, and breeding places. Weaker individuals are forced to live in poorer areas with less food, and some do not survive. The offspring of dominant parents also have the best chances of survival. The traits of the strongest individuals are thus passed on to the next generation of the species.

Stress occurs among crowded or suddenly altered populations of plants and animals. Members of a stressed plant population may go into shock and become susceptible to rapidly spreading diseases and parasites, reducing the size of the population. Members of a stressed animal population become aggressive and irritable, and they frequently fight with one another. Some individuals do not breed, and those that do breed produce smaller litters. Stressed females do not take care of their young, and may even eat their offspring.

Niche

If we think of the habitat of an organism as its "address", we can think of the niche as its "profession". The ecological niche of an organism depends not only on where it lives but also on what its role is in the forest community (how it transforms energy, behaves, responds to and modifies its physical and biotic environment), and how it relates to other species.

Ecologist Eugene P. Odum puts it this way: "If we wished to become acquainted with some person in our human community we would need to know, first of all, his address, that is, where he could be found. To really get to know him, however, we would have to learn more than the neighborhood where he lives or works. We would want to know something about his occupation, his interests, his associates, and the part he plays in general community life. So it is with the study of organisms; learning the habitat is just the beginning. To determine the organism's status in the natural community we would need to know something of its activities, especially its nutrition and energy source; also its rate of metabolism and growth, its effect on other organisms with which it comes into contact, and the extent to which it modifies or is capable of modifying important operations in the ecosystem." *

---

*E. P. Odum, *Fundamentals of Ecology*, 3rd Edition, 1971, pp. 233-234; W. B. Saunders Co., Philadelphia, Pennsylvania.

Upsetting the Balance

These are the factors you need to consider for sensitive and sensible forest management. Major changes sometimes alter the relationships within natural communities. When such changes occur, entire populations may be wiped out or may grow at an astounding rate. Some of these changes result from natural disasters, such as fires and floods. But many have resulted from thoughtless human actions such as massive elimination of plants and animals. Keep these factors in mind as you make decisions in your forest management — if you think about each one before you act, you can take steps to maintain, not disrupt, the balance of Nature.

Study and learn all you can about the various plants and animals you are interacting with. Learn what their needs and their natural checks are, and use these natural checks in your management to obtain the desired results.

Forest Succession / Climax

Forest succession is a series of relatively orderly changes that occur very slowly over periods of many years, as new types of systems in nature gradually replace, or succeed, old ones. There may be one or several intermediate stages in a succession, for it may take thousands of years for a succession to be completed. As the succession proceeds, the organisms and their habitats change with their surroundings. Differences in light intensity, protection from wind, and changes in soil may alter the kinds of organisms in an area, and may determine how many can live there. Then, as the kinds of plants and animals change, the environment itself changes. This final stage of succession is called the climax. It usually lasts for thousands of years.

A forest fire, or a harvesting practice, for example, may start a new succession beginning with flowers and grasses, then a succession of shrubs and various species of trees until finally a climax forest is reached where one plant species dominates for generation after generation. In southwestern Oregon some of the Douglas-fir forests have been in a climax stage for thousands of years.

Before you begin harvesting in a given management unit in your forest, you must determine what ecological stage the forest is in. In particular, you have to decide whether the forest is still undergoing succession or whether it has reached a climax stage. You must also determine in which layer of the forest the crowns of each species will mature. You should be able to tell by observation which population will ultimately succeed in becoming dominant, and whether one population is necessary in order to provide an adequate environment for the other. For example, if the canopy dominants in a particular

*The forest moves into a meadow. First a man-
zanita community develops, then an oak community, and finally a climax Douglas-fir
forest in the background.*

forest community are madrones but most of the seedlings on the
forest floor are Douglas-fir, then you know this forest community is
in succession — in time, the firs will replace the madrones.

Since only green plants can make their own food and therefore
all other plants and animals depend on green plants for their food, it
follows that the dominant plants will be the major controlling factor
in the composition of the forest community. In a forest with given
climate, soil, and water conditions, many different kinds of plants
may be able to grow. Their genetic traits, however, will eventually
determine which ones will become canopy dominants. The canopy
dominants will then control the forest community structure. They do
this by first controlling the climate below the forest canopy as well as
changing the soil and water conditions. They can then control the
plant community itself from the understory down to the forest floor.

The dominants may control only for a generation, until they
have modified the climate to such an extent that they cannot

regenerate their own kind — this is a forest in succession. Or the dominants may provide climate, soil and water conditions which support their own regeneration — in other words, a climax forest. In either case, the dominants of the forest canopy control the kinds of plants that can live in that forest community.

Because the climate controls which species of plants can live in the forest layers, the single most important — and most controllable — factor to consider when harvesting is the climate established within each of the forest layers. You can determine with a fair degree of accuracy what the climate requirement is for each plant by imagining what it would feel like to you if you were to be where it normally grows during extremes in summer and winter weather. Observe sunlight, temperature, wind, and the availability of water. Visualize, within each forest layer, what the temperature would feel like to you, how moist the soil and air would be, how much of the sun's rays would strike you, how much wind would hit you, and the temperature of the soil. Then decide whether your proposed harvesting action will alter the climate favorably or unfavorably.

If you harvest in a manner that severely changes the forest climate, you will upset the system of checks and balances in the forest community. This will cause some plant and animal populations to soar while others disappear. You can easily observe this occurence in and around areas of a forest where a clear cut has been made. Old varieties of plants and animals often disappear while new ones quickly emerge and dominate. You will observe many trees dying around the area because of a dramatic increase in the number of insects — insects that were once friends of the forest in that they helped remove the less healthy trees to make room for the stronger dominants. The birds used to check the insect population, but the birds are gone because their habitat has been destroyed. More insects will need more trees to feed on, and so they will keep multiplying until there is a check on their population growth. When food supply is their only check, insects can sometimes destroy an entire forest.

You must be continually aware that poor harvesting methods can severely alter the forest climate and create a devastating impact upon certain forms of wildlife which, in turn, can upset the natural system of checks and balances within the forest community. Sometimes even the removal of a single tree can have a major impact on the area beneath and immediately around it, particularly on a south slope where climate conditions may be more severe. The profit gained in harvesting the wrong trees can be offset many times over by the costs of management until another crop is ready.

Natural Selection

Natural selection in the forest is a process in nature by which the organisms best suited to their environment are the ones most likely to survive. Charlie Darwin called this process "survival of the fittest." The theory of natural selection is based on the great variation among individuals of a species, even closely related individuals. In most cases, no two members are exactly alike. Each has a unique combination of such traits as size, shape, color, and ability to withstand temperature extremes. Most of these traits are inherited. Plants and animals produce many offspring, some of which die before they can reproduce. Natural selection is the process in nature that determines which members of a species (or, which traits in a species) will survive and continue and which will not.

In the forest the necessities of life — sunlight, space, food, water, etc. — are in limited supply, so living organisms must constantly compete for them. They must also struggle against such dangers as animals that prey on them, or unfavorable weather. Some individuals have combinations of traits that help them in the struggle for life, while others have traits that are less suitable for a particular environment. Those with favorable traits, according to natural selection, are most likely to survive, reproduce, and pass on those traits to their young. Those individuals less able to compete are likely to die prematurely or to produce fewer or inferior offsping. Consequently, the favorable traits survive while the unfavorable ones eventually die out.

Forest succession and natural selection both involve survival of the fittest. Forest succession, however, is a term used to reflect both changes in population size and the elimination and/or introduction of populations as a result of a changing environment within the forest community. It involves a sequence of communities replacing communities. When the populations of different species stabilize, which may take millions of years, the forest is referred to as a climax forest.

Conclusions

1. Increasing the diversity of your forest products means increasing the diversity of the forest ecosystem. The key to long-term forest health is increased diversity, for this means a more complex, and hence more stable, forest ecosystem. A more stable system is more sustainable, and less prone to disruption (disease, infestation, etc.). It can also produce a greater variety of products and generate revenue not only from timber for sawlogs, but also from the sale of poles and firewood, from the use of the land for hiking and biking trails, for hunting, fishing, and camping, for mushrooms and huckleberry brush, and for forest management tours!

The forest ecosystem is very complex. If we change or remove part of the existing ecosystem, then we interrupt the interdependence and the natural checks and balances that occur between its many parts. Even if we only remove one key link in this vital system of relationships, we can totally change the ecosystem — which may result in a severe setback in the quality of our forest. Removal of too many forest products at one time, for example, can result in a change in forest climate. Sometimes the removal of a key link can result in the total loss of a forest, reverting the succession process back, for instance, to grasses or shrubs.

2. Forest climate is the foundation of forest health. To maintain a healthy forest you must address forest climate in *all* your management and harvesting techniques. Regard each tree, shrub, and plant as an ally that helps the forest in some way, even though we may not understand just how at this time. For example, the old twisted oak tree standing on the south slope may seem useless for anything but firewood ... until we notice the crowd of little Douglas-fir seedlings coming up under the protective shelter of the overhanging branches which provide both moisture and shade. Remember, also, to practice good soil and water conservation.

3. Maintain adequate habitats for all natural species of plants and animals found in a forest community. Improve water quality, streams and wildlife habitats, taking care, for example, to preserve some snags.

4. Maintain the complex food chains, the food web, that help stabilize the forest ecosystem. Avoid, if at all possible, the use of unnatural forest management methods — such as the massive use of chemicals — for the control of certain plants and animals.

5. Do not specialize in one species or even in just a few. Natural Selection Forest Management is a harvesting process that sees everything in the forest as having a role or a potential market, if not now, then sometime down the road. No part of the ecosystem is removed without careful study and good reason. As competition limits growth, the best of the more desirable species are selected to remain and be managed. This reduces management costs. Natural Selection Forest Mangement, by its very technique of harvesting, is a continual process of affordably analyzing the total forest community.

Guidelines

Slash

Avoid management and harvesting techniques that cause pollution, especially air pollution. Reduce or eliminate the costly need to burn slash. Slash burning is not only a hazard to the rest of the forest, it is also a growing source of air pollution. Anything over 2'' diameter can be cut while thinning and used for fuel or firewood, for example. Pieces under 2'' can be left on the ground to decompose. This is a key source of soil replenishment.

Harvest Frequency

Observe and maintain an ongoing analysis of the forest ecosystem and your forest's stages of ecological succession. This will help you decide how often to harvest. If you think of your standing trees as forest capital, you can think of the new wood growth on the trees as interest on that capital.

Ideally, you should harvest every year. Economics, energy and luck, however, are variables which may make yearly harvests on the same stand more ideal than real. Economics plays an important role in deciding when to harvest, and a practical compromise could be a longer harvest rotation period such as, say, five years. You can change this time period when necessary — it is primarily a guide for determining the spacing of plants during the thinning/harvesting process. This spacing affects the quantity you can harvest per acre, and consequently the economics of the harvest rotation period.

Many other factors in the forest affect the harvest rotation period. The climate, soil, and water all have a direct bearing on potential growth rates. Each species has its own growth rate and that, in turn, is affected by the forest climate in varying degrees. The condition of the total ecosystem also has an influence. And the position of each species in the process of ecological succession plays an important role as well. The more you become familiar with each species in each forest and their many relationships, the better the forest will become.

As is true with most things in life, the first time through is a learning process and is the most difficult. With time and experience you'll find it gets easier as the quality and value of your products increase with each harvest.

Genetics and Restocking

Address genetic improvement and restocking of all species through Natural Selection Forest Management. If you need to restock an area with natural restocking problems, you can often gather the best seedlings from the immediately surrounding area. These seedlings have already been genetically selected naturally, so there is little risk as to their quality and adaptability on your site. Your planting site must have a compatible environment for the species you select. If the environment has been severely altered by previous harvesting techniques, for example, then you may want to plant a less desirable species to develop the microclimate necessary to support the more desirable species at a later time. Poor management and harvesting techniques can cause ecological regression to the point where it can take a human lifetime or more to economically obtain restocking of the original species.*

When Natural Selection Forest Management is employed and permanent access roads are constructed (see Appendix), the lower road edges on hillsides can become large natural seed beds where the seedlings are genetically selected naturally at no cost. Seedlings can usually be lifted easily from the soft lower edge of these access roads. They are there when you want them, and they can be transplanted with minimum shock and failure. Another big advantage is that the soils on your proposed planting site can be easily compared for compatibility with the soils where the seedlings are located.

This method of obtaining seedlings can become a safer lower cost way to acquire genetically superior seedlings for your area than conventional nursery stock.

Natural Selection Harvesting

The key to Natural Selection Forest Management is *natural selection harvesting*. Natural selection harvesting is the continuous process of thinning and removing the weaker members of a population — as selected by nature — to allow adequate territories for the roots and crowns of the stronger dominants. The dominant members are left to survive and reproduce. When the dominants reach the end of their natural life, they will then become the weaker members and so will in turn be replaced by a new generation of dominants. Sometimes the canopy can be opened some to produce a climate suitable for seedlings. And so the cycle is repeated.

Trees do best when their crowns grow within the layer of the forest structure having the most suitable climate. Both crowns and roots have certain territorial as well as climatic needs. Obviously, roots are difficult to observe; crowns, however, are indicative of roots — if crowns have adequate growing room it is likely the roots do also. Therefore the emphasis of Natural Selection Forest Management is on the crowns.

---

*If your land has been subjected to unnatural harvesting processes in the past it may well need costly help in order to initially restock the more valuable species removed and to speed up the natural succession process from the point of ecological regression that results from unnatural harvesting. For example, if part of your land has been clearcut you may want to consider a tree farm program, such as producing Christmas trees, to accelerate regeneration and recoup some of your management costs.

Natural selection in action. Of the four trees in the center of the photograph, the tree on the left and the third from the left have been selected by nature to be dominants. The other two have been selected for eventual removal and can be harvested to serve our needs.

View the forest from the top of the canopy down to the forest floor. Those trees at the top are the dominant members of their population — selected by nature to survive. Leave these and remove others of the population to provide adequate territories for the dominants.

Once you have determined the dominant or "leave" trees, those which dominate the canopy, you can proceed with the thinning and removal of competing vegetation for all species. You will first want to remove the suppressed plants or those of poorer quality. Then you can continue with successively higher crown classes until you obtain the desired thinning. You may also want to remove the diseased and mature trees, preferably before they start to deteriorate in quality, unless it can be determined that removal will do more harm than good to the forest (e.g. by destroying habitats).

For maximum return, it may be best to tie your harvesting process to specific markets at various times (for example, Christmas trees or firewood), by only selecting those products which are marketable. However, it often takes years to correct overcrowding and sometimes, when left for too long, it may be extremely difficult to correct. So don't let your forest crowns overcrowd too long while waiting for the market to develop. Keep your forest in good health!

Spacing by Crown Cover

The area of the crown cover above the ground shows you the root area needed to support maximum growth potential. This is true for all species. In thinning and harvesting, determine spacing by the crown cover area. To assure maximum yield, maintain maximum crown cover area over the forest floor without crowding.

The rotation period you select will also determine the amount of spacing that will be needed between crowns to support each tree's maximum growth potential for that period of time. Use the previous lateral growth rate of the crowns to determine the amount of spacing they will need.

Too much thinning is probably worse than too little. Too much thinning at one time can change the forest climate and the community structure, producing a setback in the forest condition. It can even put trees into shock, opening the door to disease and insects. It can also allow large limbs to grow low down on the trunks, reducing their market value. Or trees may be left exposed to blowdown by heavy winds, whereas before they may have sheltered one another. We can see the effect of too much thinning in many harvesting operations today.

Too little thinning, on the other hand, can cause the crowns to become small and the trunks spindly in their struggle to survive. Growth rates can become extremely slow. Trees may succumb to insects and disease because of their poor health. If the crowns get too small, it may take years to bring growth up to potential; sometimes it can never be done, no matter how we thin.

Never change the forest climate too much at one time as a result of thinning. Look up and see if the crown and branches left will touch or be spaced too far apart. Also try to see what will be left to choose from during your next thinning. In an unmanaged stand, it may take several thinnings to obtain the desired results. Small crowns and trunks, for example, often require several thinnings before they can be opened up to the desired spacing for optimum growth.

Forest Management Checks

Observe and maintain an ongoing analysis of the balance of nature in your forest. Have a check system against poor management and harvesting practices. One pretty good rule is not to remove any plant unless there is a healthy plant to take its place. For example, when two trees are growing close together so that their branches overlap, if we remove the smaller, weaker tree then the stronger, larger one will have room to grow bigger and healthier. Ask yourself these questions:

1. Am I addressing forest needs first?
2. Am I asking the question, "Which plants would nature select to be removed?"
3. Is space being created for a healthy plant to take the place of the plant I intend to remove, as in Natural Selection?
4. Will the forest community be left in good health with all its checks and balances functioning well?
5. Do I feel certain of my decision? (The rule here is: "When in doubt, don't!" Get expert advice or evaluate the situation until you are satisfied with what you propose to do. If you still cannot decide, it's best not to do anything).

THE FOREST MANAGEMENT PLAN

A forest management plan is the development of your forest's needs, your personal goals, and your personal restrictions into a workable and satisfying timetable. It helps you not only to plan for immediate action but also to develop a logical sequence for operations one, five, ten, twenty, even fifty years from now. In the beginning, this plan can be simple, but it will gain in detail with time, and it will change as conditions change. Any difference in forest needs, personal goals, personal restrictions, markets, practices, laws, etc., may require a change in your management plan.

From time to time you might need to relate a part of your management plan to someone else — to another forest farmer, to consulting foresters, financial backers, product purchasers, product harvesters, or technical assistants. The more thinking and planning you have done prior to seeking professional advice, the better the assistance you can get.

Personal Improvements (Property)

What personal improvement do you have on your forest land? House? Barn? Shop? Trails? Fences? Access roads? Other? How much impact have these improvements had on the forest ecosystem? The smaller the parcel of land the greater the impact of these improvements, especially below 160 acres.

Equipment Needs

The kind of equipment you need will first depend on your goals and then on your restrictions. Will you manage your forest yourself or will someone else do it for you? It will also depend on the kinds of forest species you are managing, on their size, on the terrain you are working with, and on the accessibility to each of your various forest products.

Light equipment could include tools such as chainsaws, repair tools, axes, wedges, measuring tapes, and fire extinguishers. Heavy equipment might include, for example:

- a 4-wheel drive pickup
- a winch mounted on a crawler, wheel tractor, or truck, etc., to remove logs and other products from the forest
- skidding equipment to transport logs and other products to a truck loading area
- loading equipment
- a truck to transport forest products to market.

If you have a well-designed access road system (see Appendix), you can get by with a minimum of heavy equipment. Find out what equipment other forest farmers in your area are using. Your local Forest Farm or Small Woodlands Association can be an invaluable source of information on what works well in your area.

Inventory

You should find out how many different kinds of "forest communities" you have, and how many acres you have in each type. There is a special low-cost method of taking forest inventory designed especially to serve the needs of the forest farmer using Natural Selection Forest Management. Here is one way to do it: Identify common types of forest communities. The kinds of products within any area and their sizes should be about the same. From this you can easily take inventory of a small plot or two to project your total inventory of any specific product. If you have been managing for some time, your experience will give you a good idea of what you have.

There are certain conditions that can change your usable inventory for marketing: (1) access roads, (2) forest needs, (3) areas along streams, (4) rock outcroppings, (5) swamps, (6) steepness of slopes, (7) aspect (direction of slope, e.g. north or south), (8) past management practices, (9) personal considerations, (10) land developments, (11) deed restrictions, (12) land use planning, and (13) taxation (land, income and, particularly, the severance tax).

By identifying forest communities with the same forest structure and age categories, you will be able to: (1) know what you have in your forest structure, (2) manage for the forest's needs, (3) identify areas with common species, (4) locate products of a certain size, (5) determine the kinds of equipment that will be necessary for harvesting, (6) allow for a quick inventory for a specific market, (7) remove products quickly for small markets (if adequate access roads have been developed).

48

This inventory should also point out areas with access or other management restrictions, because their forest communities will be different.

Projected Average Annual Yield

Projecting an average annual yield of all products for a new forest farm is tough. All yield tables I know of are based on monocultural management programs. Ecologists know we can obtain more fibre per acre on a mixed stand because there is less competition, and with Natural Selection Forest Management there is always high productivity.

The best way to determine your projected annual yield is from past experience and records. If there are no records, you can take the following approach: categorize your various forest communities on an aerial photograph by defining the areas with common dominants and then those with trees of the same ages. After you have determined the acreages within each community category, take sample plots to determine what species are there, their size, and their values. Then on the basis of your decision as to what should come out now and what next year, and each year thereafter, you can project an average annual yield.

Often, however, it is best just to start harvesting as needed, and eventually — with experience behind you — you can establish some reasonable figures.

Timetable

Marketing is the key to your timetable for the harvesting of all products. If you can find reasonable markets for your products, it then becomes fairly easy to establish a timetable. Since most of your management is a harvesting program tied to marketing your products, it needs to be an ongoing annual program. If your personal restrictions keep you from doing that, then you may need some help.

Market

For every product there is a market; many products have several potential uses and markets. Forest farming success hinges on your ability to (1) recognize the potential of various products, (2) connect with those who would purchase them, and (3) get them to the buyers in the form that they want.

Reforestation

If your forest land is healthy, you should not need to plant trees or other forest plants. Many forest land owners, however, have inherited the consequences of poor forest management and harvesting practices: unhealthy or devastated forests. If this is your case, you may want to replant the forest and then use various agricultural methods to restore it more rapidly than Nature would. If the climate, soil, and water conditions have been changed too drastically, however, neither you nor Nature may be able to restore it. If this is the case and you wish to turn to tree farming, there is plenty of information available from conventional forestry information sources.*

Fire Protection

In Oregon, the State Forestry Department will tell you what fire-fighting tools you need for your specific operation. Forest fires can be devastating. They can put you out of business in just a few hours and destroy your home along with your forest. You should always be aware of the forest's vulnerability to fire, especially during dry seasons, and take the necessary precautions. Having the necessary tools to meet state requirements is a good start. The contour access road system I have developed (see Appendix) is one of the best deterrents against a disastrous forest fire because it is a good fire break system — plus it allows quick and easy access to the fire.

Energy

You can fulfill all of your energy needs from the forest, but some are not yet practical. A practical energy source is the use of firewood for heating. One cord of good dry firewood burned in a reasonably efficient stove has the heating ability of about 175 gallons of oil. If oil costs $1.00 per gallon, then a cord of wood should be worth $175.00 in comparable heat. Firewood is a by-product of Natural Selection

---

*There is also plenty of excellent material available from unconventional forestry information sources. Some of the best references are: (1) *Tree Crops (A Permanent Agriculture)*, by J. Russell Smith; Harper & Row: 1950; (2) *Forest Farming*, by J. S. Douglas and R. A. Hart; Rodale, Emmaus, PA: 1976; (3) *Permaculture One* and *Two*, by Bill Mollison; International Tree Crops Institute, Winters, CA: 1978,79; (4) *Tree Talk*, by Ray Raphael; Island Press, Covelo, CA: 1981; (5) *Agroforestry Review*, PO Box 666, Winters, CA 95694; (6) *Forest Planning*, PO Box 3479, Eugene, OR 97403. A standard conventional reference is *The Woodland Handbook for the Pacific Northwest*, Oregon State University Extension Service: 1974.

Forest Management and so lends itself beautifully to your operation. Firewood can not only serve all your own heating needs but also other needs such as power generation and engine fuels.*

Records

You need an adequate bookkeeping system to keep you informed of your progress and to provide the necessary information for tax purposes. You will need to record the kinds of products sold, the dates, amounts received, amounts paid out in expenses, investments in equipment, road costs, structures, taxes, etc. You may want to consult an accountant familiar with forestry to help you set up your books.

Community Asset

When you have drafted your forest management plan be sure to ask yourself these questions:

- Is my forest management plan a continuous asset to the forest?
- Does my forest management plan address my personal goals without seriously interfering with the forest's needs?
- Does my forest management plan adequately *integrate* management considerations for addressing the forest's needs, my personal goals, and my personal restrictions?
- Does my forest management plan address the ecological and social needs of the other people in the watershed where I live?
- Natural Selection Forest Management can allow you to answer "yes" to these questions.

---

*Articles on these subjects appear regularly in publications like *The Mother Earth News.*

CONCLUSION

Understanding the forest as a living ecosystem with its own set of natural checks and balances is the first step toward sensible management of your forest land. Once you begin to see the forest as a whole and observe its complex interdependencies, you quickly see the ecological inadequacy of harvesting trees on the basis of a monocultural model. Preserving the forest environment becomes a primary goal not only to benefit ecological health but also because it is more profitable in the long-term as well. Using all of the products the forest has to offer spreads the profitable harvests over a diversity of goods and therefore protects the forest environment and keeps it intact. If forest products are harvested according to Natural Selection Forest Management, then the forest itself can be used in a variety of ways.

Our forests are indeed our greatest natural resource, and therefore we clearly have a responsibility to protect them. As forest farmers we can also make a difference in the way public forests are managed, and it is important that we do so.

Congress passed the Multiple-Use, Sustained Yield Act on June 12, 1960. Some 25 years later, however, we see that government foresters are looking primarily at sustained *timber* yield rather than at sustained *forests*. They cannot hope to sustain forests if timber is the main emphasis and the rest of the forest is considered incidental. The emphasis should be on sustained forests with timber as only one of many products. Only then could the end result be a sustained yield for timber. Likewise, if our forests were genuinely managed for multiple use — managed for all forest products and forest uses — both forest needs and human needs would be better served.

My home state of Oregon has to date only taken advantage of two of its forests' many products and uses: (1) the conifer trees and their related products, and (2) recreation and tourism. All the other forest products are left for the most part untapped, and most are even destroyed by burning or the massive use of chemicals. This is a foolish and destructive situation we find ourselves in.

Who is responsible for this dilemma? We have seen how confusing definitions of forestry practices led to laws prejudiced in favor of the timber industry. We have seen how present-day taxation rates put an unjust hardship on the forest farmer. We have seen how forestry schools train foresters for the timber industry, not for the forest. We have seen how land use planning needs to be directed towards the preservation of forest land to prevent widespread real estate development from destroying this valuable natural resource. And we have seen how present forestry practices on public forest lands are both impractical and destructive, and how they affect our private forests.

Perhaps one of the greatest threats to the private forest industry today is the real estate speculators and developers. They are making a lot of money at the expense of private forestry and the public by converting forest resource land into developments that consume those resources and impact adjoining forests. If the developments continue as in the past, it is only a matter of time before there will be no more private forestry. It will only be government forestry — and now the pressure is on to develop that, too!

The creation in Oregon of the State Land Conservation and Development Commission (LCDC) was an attempt to preserve natural resources such as forests — however, LCDC has not been able to adequately define forestry, let alone administer a policy. The real estate people have conducted an enormous campaign aimed at discrediting LCDC in Oregon, arguing that LCDC exists to strip away the rights of the public, rather than to preserve those rights. Yet it is interesting to note that in land use planning the restrictions necessary for preserving our rights (to life, liberty, and the pursuit of happiness) are always greater on residential development lands than on forest resource lands. In fact, when forest resource lands are converted to residential development lands, individuals necessarily lose some of their personal rights, except the right to further develop land! The right to manage a forest, like other personal rights, becomes secondary to the right to develop property for other uses (e.g. housing), and so any forest management that may become a nuisance to adjoining property owners, such as the sound of equipment noises, is no longer allowed.

In the county I live in, for example, where most of the land is forest land, the real estate speculators and developers are running rampant over the forest. Much of our forest land has perhaps more potential diversity of natural forest products than most any forest land in the nation — yet it is being removed (cut, paved, developed) on a mass scale.

Private non-industrial forest farmers — that's us — have not been able to compete against the short-term profit drive of the real estate speculators and developers, who include the private non-industrial forest owners out to sell their land (and when they sell, they can often make more quick money by subdividing and developing). LCDC has been the forest farmer's only ally, but the realty developers and promoters have used their big bucks to render LCDC largely ineffective, leaving the private non-industrial forest farmers — you and me — to fight development with our own time and money. If we win, it will be years before we realize the benefits. If the speculators and developers of our forest resource lands win, we will all lose.

How effective land use planning is at protecting forest land from development for other uses will depend on local, state, and national policies. I do not believe, based on my own experience, that it can be adequately accomplished on any one level. It requires a good working relationship among all these levels. The whole reason for planning seems to be circumvented by special interest groups if any one level is not doing its part.

The history of forests in other countries has shown that people can indeed wipe out an entire forest, leaving only a desert and widespread poverty. If we are to achieve a more positive outcome, we must first practice good forestry on our own lands. Then we must begin to educate others concerned with forestry, to tell them what we have learned about these forestry practices, to demonstrate their worth. Organizations of forest farmers, such as the Forest Farm Associations in southern Oregon, are invaluable to us. It is only with the spread of an ecological understanding among foresters, and of the management practices that result from this understanding, that we can save our forests for future profit and enjoyment.

55

APPENDIX: Access Roads

You need a good access road system for economical harvesting and marketing of your forest products. You may also need access roads to serve other purposes such as recreation and enjoyment. You must weigh the impact your roads will have upon the forest in terms of erosion problems, water and stream pollution, destruction of wildlife habitat and shelter, and so forth. Access roads are a necessary compromise between the forest's needs and our needs if we are to successfully make use of forest products. That is not to say that all forests need roads, nor is it to say that none should have them. To have useful access roads without inflicting serious damage on the forests requires very careful design and construction. You'll want roads of the minimum size and impact possible for you to accomplish your goals, and you'll want to avoid access roads in areas with extremely steep slopes, unstable soils, swamps, rock outcroppings, near streambeds, and special habitat areas.

The cost of building roads in such areas is very high anyway, so foregoing those roads in favor of the forest ecosystem is a small price to pay. I find that when forest needs are addressed first and human needs second, there is a natural moderation in access roads with the result that human needs are best served as well.

What are the *advantages* of a good road system that gives complete access to your forest?

- It allows immediate access to any size product, large or small, when a market develops for it.
- It creates a minimum impact on the forest during harvest operations.
- It increases the value of all your forest products by reducing harvesting and marketing costs.
- It provides access for fire protection, and serves as fire breaks during a fire. Contour access roads provide elaborate fire breaks.

- It can make year-round harvesting possible, enabling you to remove products when it will have the least impact on the forest and when the market and prices are the best.
- It can enable you to economically remove small special products.
- It allows you to have a sustained annual income.
- It can allow you to use smaller, less costly equipment, creating less impact on the forest.
- It allows for quick inventory for any special market.
- It helps you attain more yield and variety of products per acre.
- It can, with careful design and construction, substantially reduce erosion problems.

What are the *disadvantages* of a permanent forest access road system?
- Initial cost in terms of money for construction.
- Some unavoidable impact on your forest, although if the roads are properly designed and constructed, it should be less than that of most access road systems commonly used in forestry today.
- The necessity of a maintenance program. If you do not live on your farm, you may not be able to spot problems (such as water coming from unexpected places) early enough to prevent costly damange. If you do live on the parcel and can observe your road system easily, when a high water condition erupts you may be able to solve a potentially major problem with no more than a shovel. Whether you have a major or minimum cost in road maintenance will depend primarily on such factors as how well the road is designed and constructed, what it is used for, how much, with what kind of equipment, and during what kind of weather. Proper design and construction are the keys to minimum maintenance.

Costs

You may need to invest in a good access road system to make your forest farm economically viable. Typical government figures for forest access road costs start at about $10,000 per mile and run to $100,000 and more for design and construction. In contrast to this, the kinds of access roads that forest farmers in my area have been typically using, such as contour access roads, do not come to $10,000 per mile even under the most difficult conditions unless there are other special considerations such as bridges, very large culverts, very hard rock, or switchbacks on steep ground. The major factor, often overlooked, is the kind of surface the road will need. The difference between a surface for seasonal use and one designed for year-round use can easily double the road cost.

Kind Of Access Road System

If you are inexperienced with forest farming, you have probably not given much thought to your access road system, taking it for granted that when it comes to harvesting, there will be some type of equipment available to get your products out. And it is true that regardless of the situation, there most likely is *some* kind of equipment that can economically remove the larger timber products. But what about the smaller products and future harvests?

As the owner or long-term manager of the forest, you must look at a *continual* harvesting of a variety of forest products, as well as other forest uses. Your forest farm will require an access road system that caters to not only the largest products but also the smallest, as well as to many other uses. You must also consider the fact that your access road system needs to accomodate an annual harvesting program instead of the once or twice in a lifetime harvests of most conventional management programs.

I have developed a low-cost, minimum-impact road access system, called a "Contour Access System," based on the agricultural concept of plowing fields perpendicular to the direction of water runoff. I try to avoid, if at all possible, the typical "skid roads" that run parallel to the water drainage, and so I also avoid most serious erosion problems. The roads slow down runoff water and perhaps even store a little during times of drought. This is the most economical and ecologically sensible road system I know of.

Road Placement

If you have flat land, you may be able to put your roads anywhere you like, but if your forest grows on hills you will have to design your road system more carefully. On my forest farm the road spacing is 150-200 feet. You can design your road system along the lines of a Douglas-fir tree, the trunk being the primary road system for trucking all of your forest products to market, and the branches representing small secondary roads for gathering those products. These small secondary roads will serve to move large products, such as saw logs, to the primary road where a large truck can transport them to market. For smaller hand-carried products, such as firewood, small vehicles like pickups can load and transport directly from these secondary roads. This can give immediate economical access to any forest product, large or small, whenever a market occurs, and can allow harvesting with very little impact to the forest ecosystem.

Road Types

There are four basic kinds of roads: flat, crowned, in-sloped, and out-sloped. The main difference between the four road types is in the way they handle water on the road surface. Each has its advantages and disadvantages.

Flat roads are the cheapest and easiest to construct, and with limited use they have the least impact upon the forest. They require less width and few or no culverts and are especially well suited to steep slopes on secondary roads because of their minimal hillside cut requirements. However, they hold water on the road, a very serious problem that causes serious maintenance problems if used when they are wet.

Outsloped roads overcome this problem. The disadvantage of out-sloped roads is that they are of limited value during wet weather. Water runs across them from the hillside above, and if the road is slick you may slide off with the water!

In-sloped roads, on the other hand, overcome the dangerous part of sliding over the mountain by tipping the road toward the upper hillside. However, this creates other problems. They catch the water, thus requiring the installation of somewhat costly culverts. Higher maintenance costs and water pollution problems can also occur by using vehicles during rainy seasons.

Crowned and ditched roads require the least amount of maintenance but are the most expensive to construct. Though they are used throughout the country, they are not always the best road for the job in the forest because they require more width. On steep slopes, for example, they may create a much greater impact on the forest than an in- or out-sloped secondary road of limited usage.

A well-designed forest access road system in the mountains may use a combination of all three road types depending on water conditions, usage, cost, and forest impact. For year-round use, a good crowned, ditched road system with good culverts is a necessity, and in the long run it is the least costly kind of primary road system.

Road Width

The maximum width normally allowed on highway vehicles such as log-ging trucks is 8 feet. Logging trucks are the largest vehicles you will need to accomodate on your primary road system. If you allow a 2' buffer on either side this gives you a 12'-wide surface area for a straight road. On turns you will need to allow for trailers and may require 20 feet or more, depending on the sharpness of the turn and on the partiuclar trucks involv-ed.

Sharp turns, such as switchbacks, require a certain minimum radius. A well-designed logging truck can usually turn around a 50' radius. You will need to check this out for your locale.

Secondary roads are not designed for logging trucks but rather for skidding long logs with heavy equipment. They are also designed for smaller trucks so they can be narrower.

Design Your Road System For Your Equipment

You should design your road system for the smallest sized equipment that will economically do the job for you. The smaller the equipment, the smaller the roads, and subsequently the less impact on your forest.

Road size will be determined by the largest products that will be harvested and the size of equipment necessary to handle them. On a primary road system, it is usually a logging truck that transports your logs to market. On secondary roads, size is determined by the weight of the equipment necessary to handle the largest products. While different types of forest may require some variations in sizing, primary roads that do not require vehicles to pass one another except in turnouts can usually be as narrow as 12 feet.

Maximum and Minimum Grades

If you have a forest on mountainsides, you will need to consider max-imum grade. Road grades are commonly expressed in percentages. A 10% grade, for example, means that for 100 feet of horizontal distance the road would rise or fall 10 feet in elevation. I try to keep grades at 10% or less. I try to keep around a minimum grade of 3% on mountain roads where I can. (If you lay out your own road, you will need a clinometer or com-parable instrument for determining grade.)

Roads that are too steep have maintenance problems because wheels kick out the dirt and gravel instead of packing it. They may also be inaccessible during winter if they are slick. In mountainous forests, I like to keep some slope to the road so that water can drain off from the tracks, and maintenance problems will be reduced. Also, if you maintain a constant grade, particularly in the direction of travel for a loaded truck, much smaller equipment can be used to move the same load.

Start With Your Primary Road System

From your primary road system, determine what spot on your property is the most difficult to get to and start working your road system out from there to your destination. If you can, keep your roads sloped downhill for loaded vehicles until you reach a good, well-maintained road system. This will help you immensely during winter when roads may be slick or soft.

Aerial photos can be a big help. By working out various options on a map instead of on the ground you can save a lot of time. With the aid of an aerial photo, determine the points on the ground where a road is needed or must go. These points then determine where the rest of the road will be. Consider all possible variations and then pick the best one to serve you and your forest's needs. Notice obvious places to avoid such as swamps, streams, hard rock formations, very steep slopes, unstable soils, etc.

Now establish as many points as possible where a road must go, including property entrance, certain low impact stream crossings, property lines, etc. In mountainous forests, roads may be needed on ridges where property lines cross (if water drainage is away from your property) or in canyons where property lines cross (if drainage is toward your land). If you determine the obvious points where a road must go and those areas where it must not go, the rest of the road will design itself for you.

Dead-Ends and Turnarounds

Dead-end roads, particularly dead-end primary roads, are undesirable. If you must have a dead-end road, you will have to construct a turn-around large enough for the largest vehicle that will use the road.

One main reason for not having dead-end main roads is that you will be using them continuously for taking inventory, for checking the forest condition, and probably for recreation. It is nice when driving or walking along a road not to have to return by the same path you came on. It also makes for better use of your time.

Turnouts

You will need adequate turnouts and other areas for the preparation and storage of products for market, parking of vehicles, use of equipment, etc. If you have flat land, there is usually no problem with this, but mountainous forest land needs careful consideration. I pay particular attention in the layout of roads to natural "benches" (low cost areas to excavate for these landings or turnouts) and try to design the road system to accommodate them. Large excavations on the side of a steep mountain are very costly to both the forest and your pocketbook. For the money it may cost you to build one wide area on the side of a steep mountain, you can build a lot of road. In certain situations, however, you may need to have some landings close to your harvesting points. You then need to weigh the initial cost of the landings against the long-term cost of transporting your products to your landings.

Constructing Your Own Access Road System

The importance of how your forest access road system is laid out and constructed cannot be emphasized enough. A poorly constructed access road system can be worse than none at all, and worse still, you may have to live with it forever.

Unless you are a professional road builder and have the kind of equipment to do the job, contract it out. The problem here, however, is that most road builders do not understand the forest, let alone what harvesting entails, and those that do understand the forest and harvesting often do not understand roads and their construction. It is therefore very important to have a good understanding of your needs and your forest's needs, or to hire someone who understands all-age, all-species Natural Selection Forest Management and harvesting techniques.

Though it is desirable to construct your road system all at once, it is not necessary. You can do it when it is convenient, such as just before harvesting an area, or else when it is economically feasible, as long as you lay out your primary road first to the most difficult area it will need to serve. Remember that your primary road must be compatible with your complete road system.

Avoid temporary roads! The time and money spent on a temporary road is usually better spent on construction of a permanent one, and further temporary roads become a burden later. Make your time and money count.

Disposing of Brush, Stumps, and Other Debris

Conventional road construction methods call for the piling and burning of debris. This can add a significant cost to your road construction. If you own flat land, there is little choice. If you own forest on hillsides, you can take advantage of the lower side fill on roads and canyons by dozing stumps and other debris carefully into the bottom edge of the fill so that they will be covered over when the road excavation is complete (be careful to prevent wood from surfacing in the finished road during excavation).

Placing this debris in the lower footing of a road fill substantially stabilizes the fill, especially during the first winter after construction. Furthermore, it allows more stability for much steeper fills if necessary. I have used this approach very successfully on steep ground where I could not build up the outside edge in any other manner; otherwise it would have required a much greater cut into the hillside and a much greater impact on the forest.

Success in using debris in road fill depends on many factors, including the mixture of soil with the debris during placement and a good operator who can sense where it will be when the road is finished.

Rock and Roads

The need for rock on your roads is determined by the kind of usage and the kind of soil. You will probably need to rock your primary road system. Secondary roads are less critical; however, if you are to operate year around, you may eventually need to rock them, too.

Many forest farmers with large acreages have rock sources on their own property that they find during the course of road construction. Others may not be so fortunate.

Rocking of roads can become more costly than construction of the roads themselves so you should be aware of this hidden cost!

AFTERWORD

Although the primary purpose of this book is to enable the forest farmer to harvest in an ecologically and economically sound manner, its impact could be far greater. If Natural Selection Forest Management were widely adopted it could change our society's concepts of forests and forest management. We could learn to "see the forest through the trees."

The implications of natural selection harvesting and the other ecological methods of forest farming go beyond one's private business. Our public forests are in need of better management practices than those that industrial and public foresters have used in the past. Many of those forestry methods still common with the Bureau of Land Management and the U.S. Forest Service are destructive to the forest environment and therefore to an economy centered around timber and the forests. Some of these practices along with their objections and remedies are listed below:

(1) Monoculturally based operations treat the forest as a tree farm, following an agricultural model. At harvest, the trees may be cut down like a crop of hay. By the time the area is replanted, a year or more of growing time has been lost, and many more years will pass before it can produce its potential yield of fibre per acre. However, we know that there is less competition in any given area between trees of different species than there is between trees of the same species. A natural forest, where different species are growing, will therefore produce more gross fibre than the same area planted as a monocultural operation. I beleve that on the average, Natural Selection Forest Management could easily achieve twice the yield of a standard monocultural operation.

(2) Slash-burning is the most usual method for removing the debris left in the wake of logging operations from the forest floor and for minimizing fire hazard. Not only does this cost time and

money, but much material usable by the forest or as sellable products is lost. With Natural Selection Forest Management we remove slash down to 2" for firewood or other useful purposes. Any remaining slash the decomposers on the forest floor remove for us. This improves the soil and eliminates both the expense of burning and the hazard of fire.

(3) The massive use of herbicides and pesticides in our forests is costly and dangerous not only to the forest but to human health as well. When we consider the forest as an ecosystem, we can see that herbicides and pesticides have no place there. If a forest is healthy and has been properly harvested using natural selection management techniques, it should not require any herbicides or pesticides, as nature keeps an adequate system of checks and balances.

(4) Reforestation costs in public forests are enormous. According to the National Forest Service, the cost of reforestation in Washington and Oregon is $382 per acre. In some regions of the country, it runs as high as $893. In addition, reforestation is often not successful on land that has been severely damaged, such as clear-cut areas. Natural Selection Forest Management, by keeping an all-age stand, lets Nature plant the seedlings.

(5) Many conventional forest management tools cause severe environmental damage, which could be greatly reduced by the methods outlined in this book. For instance, small-scale harvesting equipment can cause less erosion and stream pollution than large-scale equipment, and thus can more easily maintain the forest's ability to function as a healthy organism. Natural selection management practices could eliminate these thorns in the side of public foresters. The diversity of the forest ecosystem is the key to the stability of the forest and could be the key to the stability of the timber industry as well. The reduction or elimination of management costs for reforestation and the use of chemicals would reduce the budget (our tax money) and free up the money for hiring people to fill jobs created by increased product diversity and the methods of Natural Selection Forest Management.

If natural selection harvesting practices and other methods of forest farming were to reach into our public forests as well as our own, our total forest ecosystem could become healthy as well as productive. The importance of good stewardship is obvious to forest farmers — they must learn enough about the *particular* forest they are managing to enable them to make intelligent site-specific management decisions. What about stewardship on our public lands?

Stewardship of public lands could become widespread. No forester I know of likes to manage the forest from a desk in a city office. They, too, prefer to be in the forest because they like the forest. And no one, much less the taxpayer, can afford to have government foresters spend most of their time driving down the road just to get to and from the forest. Under the stewardship concept each forester would be assigned a parcel of land, say perhaps 2000 acres (more or less depending on its productivity), to live on and caretake. Perhaps some areas might be leased to private foresters. In any case, the resident forest stewards would do all the necessary management prescriptions, lay out sales, compete with other forest managers, and, in short, be responsible for this land the same way a private forest owner is. This would allow foresters to become personally and intimately involved with their own pieces of land and would provide excellent stewardship of our forests.

The implications of forest farming by Natural Selection Forest Management could indeed be far-reaching and exciting.

Orville Camp knows forest farming as it truly is — a way of life for himself and his family. He has been studying and experimenting with both conventional and innovative forest management practices for many years. Camp has developed a system of sustainable forest management based only upon natural processes. In 1978 Camp's success in forest farming was acknowledged by the Illinois Valley Soil and Water Conservation District, which awarded him "Farmer of the Year" for outstanding woodland management. In 1979 he was named "Tree Farmer of the Year" for both Josephine and Jackson Counties. In 1980 Camp became President of the newly formed Illinois Valley Forest Farm Association, a position he held until 1983. At the same time, in 1981, he served as President of the Jackson-Josephine Forest Farm Association.

ABOUT THE EDITOR

Mark Roseland is a nationally known editor and writer. He is also Co-Director of the Matrix Institute, a non-profit center for research, education, and information on ecologically appropriate technologies and lifestyles, located in Applegate, Oregon.

ABOUT THE BOOK

Editor: *Mark Roseland*
Publisher: *SKY RIVER PRESS, Steve Bohlert*
Word Processing & Telecommunications:
 Julie Kay Norman
Photographs: *All photographs were taken on location at Camp Forest Farm, Selma, Oregon, by Dean Givens, of Dean Givens Studio, Kerby, Oregon.*
Technical Editing: *Diana Coogle*
Typeset: *This book is set in 10 point Garamond Book.*
Typesetters: *PAN TYPESETTERS of Eugene, Oregon. Text and embedded typesetting commands stored on floppy disk were transmitted via modem over common-carrier telephone lines. Sending hardware: Apple III and Smartmodem 1200. Sending Software: Applewriter III and Apple Access III. Receiving Hardware: CompuGraphic with EditWriter interface.*
Printing: *The text paper is Sundance Natural White, 70 lb. stock; the cover is Sundance Natural White, 65 lb. stock. Printing by Klocker Printery of Medford, Oregon.*